CRYPTOCURRENCY

A Basic Guide and Bible to Cryptocurrency

By

Stephen O'Shea

Table of Contents

INTRODUCTION	1
What is Cryptocurrency?	3
What is Bitcoin?	4
How Do Cryptocurrency Work?	6
How to Start?	7
How To Buy Bitcoin?	9
Cryptocurrency Vs Fiat Currency – What's The Difference?	11
What Is Cryptocurrency Mining?	13
Advantages & Disadvantages of Bitcoins	16
The transactions are completely anonymous and private. They are secure and irreversible. This gives fewer risks for merchants doing business.	16
Also used for money Laundering/Black Market.	17
Bitcoin is called the Future of Money as it is Non-Inflationary	17
Speculators wish to take advantages of Volatility of bitcoins. A huge recession will come in Bitcoins if it gets in the hands of speculator.	17
How Miners Create Coins And Confirm Transactions?	19
What Are Miners Doing?	28
What Is Cryptocurrency: 21st-Century Unicorn – Or The Money Of The Future?	34
Cryptocurrencies: Dawn Of A New Economy	40
What Is The Future Of Cryptocurrency?	49
Cryptocurrency, Blockchain Technology	52
BLOCKCHAIN	56

Bitcoin Wallet 61
Cryptocurrency Security 65
Cryptocurrency Services 70

INTRODUCTION

Cryptocurrency (or crypto currency) is a virtual or digital currency that uses cryptography, an encryption technique, for security. Cryptocurrency is a form of digital cash which is used as secure digital currency. They are used for a fast, direct and seamless transaction between the sender & receiver. CRYPTOcurrency is used because cryptography technique is used in the transaction process to keep the consensus records safe and secure.

Cryptography is an encrypted technique for storing and sending data in a specific form which can be read or processed only by those who are meant to read it. It is the process of converting ordinary plain text into unintelligible text cipher text (a process called encryption), then back again (known as decryption) and vice-versa so as to keep the information secret. Unless, you are an authorized user you can't read the data.

There are various types of algorithms for encryption, some common algorithms include:

Secret Key Cryptography (SKC): Only one key is used for both encryption and decryption. This is symmetric encryption.

Public Key Cryptography (PKC): Two keys are used. This encryption is also called asymmetric encryption. Anyone can access the public key and another key is the private key, which can be accessed only by the owner.

What is Cryptocurrency?

With cryptocurrency you have full control on your money. Cryptocurrency is a decentralized digital currency, which means that the transactions and emissions are not controlled by any organization or there's no central authority to validate your transactions.

Cryptocurrency transactions are anonymous, undetectable. The transactions are all validated by a cryptocurrency network. Moreover, the transactions in cryptocurrencies can be processed in a matter of seconds or minutes. Cryptocurrency is transferred between peers and confirmed in a public ledger via a process called as mining. It is transferred between peers i.e.; there is no middleman like a bank.

Stephen O'Shea

What is Bitcoin?

Bitcoin or BTC is the most popular, notable cryptocurrency and worldwide payment system. Bitcoin was the first decentralized digital currency, created in 2009. It was invented by Satoshi Nakamoto. It is accepted as a form of payment by many of companies. Because of high price value of bitcoins many people do bitcoin mining. It is also accepted by thousands of merchants worldwide.

Satoshi Nakamoto aims to change the way we think about money in general. In his announcement of Bitcoin in late 2008, Satoshi said he developed "A Peer-to-Peer Electronic Cash System."

Cryptocurrency

In simple words bitcoin is a "decentralized digital currency" which is fast and secure because of cryptography. People who create Bitcoins are called as miners. These miners are actually 'book-keepers' and 'validators' of the network. The most important Cryptocurrencies other than Bitcoin are Litecoin (LTC), Ethereum (ETH), Zcash (ZEC), Namecoin (), Swiftcoin, Dash, Ripple (XRP), Monero (XMR).

Stephen O'Shea

How Do Cryptocurrency Work?

Every single Cryptocurrency transaction involving Bitcoins is recorded in an open online ledger known as the Blockchain. A blockchain holds the entire history of a certain cryptocurrency. It keeps transparent records of digital transactions. The transactions are assembled into what are called "blocks" and there is a "chain" of "blocks" of transactions

Blockchain is a technology that supports many technologies and cryptocurrency is one of them. To prevent interfering, most of blockchain are open source and decentralized. Blockchain is the public ledger of every transaction that has been carried out in that cryptocurrency network.

Cryptocurrency is stored in digital wallets (a virtual bank account). From "cryptocurrency wallets" transactions are sent between peers, matching up public codes which relate back to user-held private passwords (AKA cryptographic "keys"). All the transactions are recorded in a blockchain.

How to Start?

When buying cryptocurrency for the first time you should consider some factors as mentioned below to make the right decision and choose the right platform suitable to your requirements.
- **How much privacy you can disclose?**
- **How do you want to pay?**
- **Your place of location.**

In simple terms the procedure to buy bitcoins involve – choosing the right cryptocurrency, getting a crypto-wallet and then finding a bitcoin exchange. Once you find the bitcoin exchange then trade your local currency, like U.S. dollar, Indian Rupee, Dollar, Euro etc. for bitcoins and move those bitcoins into a secure Bitcoin wallet.

First of all choose a Cryptocurrency: There are a lot of different cryptocurrencies that exist in the market today. You have to choose a currency of your interest and as per its value like Bitcoin, Ethereum etc.

Second Get a Crypto-Wallet: Then you have to choose a cryptocurrency wallet where you can hold your crypto-money. There are some compatible wallets for each currency and you have to choose the best wallet as per your needs. You can simply download these wallets to your desktop, iOS and Android phone, ready to use. For long-term storage of cryptocurrency it's also worth considering a hardware wallet. You have to choose a wallet as per your chosen cryptocurrency. A bitcoin wallet contains address (es) and private key (s).

Third Buy from Exchange: Next is you have to buy your cryptocurrency. Digital Currency Exchange (DCE) – It is a cryptocurrency exchange where you can buy or sell cryptocurrencies.

Usually, purchasing cryptocurrency for the first time you have to exchanging fiat currency (such as USD, AUD or EUR etc.) to your chosen cryptocurrency.

You can buy bitcoin from an exchange or an individual. Later on you can do trading with cryptocurrency. When you buy cryptocurrency to put into your wallet (as explained in step 2 above) you have to follow an identity verification process on the exchange, deposit your payment and then you can buy your coins.

How To Buy Bitcoin?

Bitcoin transactions are saved publicly and are visible on the blockchain so you need to make sure how much private information you are sharing. With buying bitcoins. Platforms which enables users to buy or sell bitcoins need to verify the identity of their users with **Know Your Customer rules** (KYC). The amount of private information you disclose as there are different KYC policy:

- **NO KYC** – No need to show any identity document for the verification. Neither the platform nor the seller of Bitcoins knows who you are. It is comparatively, an expensive option. Buying Bitcoin without KYC is possible in some jurisdictions.
- **KYC Light** – In KYC light your payment channel and/or your phone numbers identifies you. Limited amount of bitcoins can be purchased with KYC light.
- **Full KYC** - In Full KYC a lot of information including name, phone number, your bank account, ID card, driving license, etc. documents are used to prove your identity. Different platforms needs relevant documents for verification.

The common means of making payments to buy bitcoins are – Bank Transfer, Credit Cards, Paypal, Private/Other Payment Channels.

If you want to change your fiat-money to digital cash like in Bitcoin then there are different ways you can buy bitcoins – Bitcoin ATM, Gift Cards/Vouchers, P2P markets, Commercial Exchanges/Brokers.

Cryptocurrency Vs Fiat Currency – What's The Difference?

Cryptocurrency and Fiat currency both are called money or currency. You can buy goods and services with both these currencies. Also, both of the currencies can be traded on exchanges. But there are a lot of differences between both the currencies and below table will help you understand the differences between both the currencies clearly.

Cryptocurrency	Fiat Currency
Digital way of exchanging money.	Physical way of exchanging money.
Represented by Private or public pieces of code.	Paper money or coins.
Generated by Computers through mining process.	Issued by the Government
Almost impossible to counterfeit as it is secured by cryptographic code.	Difficult to counterfeit but possible.
It is not a "legal tender" and it is not backed by a government or bank.	It is a "legal tender" backed by a "government.
As there is no involvement of government and no bank issues it, there is no interests associated with cryptocurrencies.	You can get interest payments on your fiat money.
It is decentralized and worldwide (no one can control)	It is centralized (monitored by government.

Its value is determined on the basis of the level of supply and demand.	Its value is decided by government according to market conditions.
An algorithm controls the supply. Limited Supply & has a set of maximum.	The government controls the supply and if required can be produced by the government.
You can't pay your taxes with it, instead you have to pay taxes on it.	You can pay your taxes with it.
Example of Cryptocurrencies are – BTC (Bitcoin), ETH (Ethereum) and LTC (Litecoin) etc.	Example of Fiat Currencies are - USD (US Dollar), EU (Euro) and JPY (Japanese Yen) etc.
International transfer takes few minutes.	International transfer may takes several days.
It's nearly impossible to counterfeit as there are cryptography codes for security.	Difficult to counterfeit but it's still possible.
Cryptocurrency can be acquired by the process of mining, via sales, cryptocurrency exchanges and rarely as salaries/wages.	Fiat currency can be acquired as wages & salaries, investing, performing sales, by winning lottery or prize money.

What Is Cryptocurrency Mining?

Bitcoins and other cryptocurrencies are generated through a process which is called as 'mining'. Mining is actually a validation of the transactions in the cryptocurrency networks. People who create bitcoins are called as cryptocurrency miners. So, what is cryptocurrency mining? Let's explore further.

Cryptocurrency mining, or cryptomining, is a process of mining the crypto currency. Mining here means similar to mining any precious metal but here instead of metal it's mining of cryptocurrency.

Cryptocurrency mining is an act of computing a specific value to satisfy the hash function that will complete a block in the blockchain.

For cryptocurrency mining process miners needs a computer and special software or programs to solve computationally difficult mathematical problems or puzzles to compete with their peer miners and get rewards.

Cryptocurrency mining takes a lot of processing power. In cryptocoins mining early adopters are rewarded with whatever currency they are mining for. Also known as cryptocoins mining, altcoin mining, or Bitcoin mining (for Bitcoin cryptocurrency which is the most popular). Who solves the puzzle and provides the right answer gets the reward.

By using cryptographic hash functions the miners attempt to solve a block, after regular interval of time, which contains the transaction data. Anyone can become a miner in the network.

Cryptocurrency mining involves 2 functions: adding transactions to the blockchain (securing and verifying) and also releasing new currency. The bitcoin mining procedure goes like this - Transactions are bundled in a block. Verify, to check if transactions are valid. Select and insert the header of the recent block into a new block as a hash. Solve the proof of work problem. On finding the solution add a new block is added to the blockchain and propagated to the network.

In easy way, cryptocurrency mining is the procedure of solving blockchains that contains the information on worldwide transactions. To prevent fraud the transactions are stored on all computers that are registered as miners.

Let's understand mining with an example in more easy way:

Let's suppose I want to transfer money from my bank account in India to an account Located in US. I will transfer the amount from my account to yours from the bank I have account in.

The bank here is a third party and it maintains our account, balances i.e. our ledger. Now, the bank will take a certain percentage of the amount transferred as a fees for providing the services. The services here are of transfer of money from one account to another as well as maintenance of ledger i.e. database.

In case of cryptocurrencies there is no single entity as a banks for managing the database and transferring the amount. Cryptocurrency such as bitcoin are based on open-source blockchain technology with distributed database.

Here, the database of all the transactions that occur on the bitcoin network are maintained by the miners. The miners share their hash values and verifies transactions on the network to get rewards as bitcoin. This is how new bitcoins are generated.

Stephen O'Shea

Advantages & Disadvantages of Bitcoins

ADVANTAGES	DISADVANTAGES
Direct transfer from person to person.	Each transaction logs is shared publicly online resulting in privacy & security concerns.
Low/ minimal transaction fees when you pay through bitcoin. To process the transactions faster you can include your fees and higher fees gives it priority.	Not refundable or replaceable. Lack of standardized policy for chargebacks or refunds.
Payment freedom - Send/receive money anywhere in the world at any time. No intermediaries in between.	Lack of awareness & understanding about digital currencies and Bitcoin.
You are in control of your money with Bitcoin.	Bitcoins are limited amount of coins so it has volatility.
The transactions are completely anonymous and private. They are secure and irreversible. This gives fewer risks for merchants doing business.	A lot of business are not ready to accept bitcoin as a payment method.

Cryptocurrency

With bitcoin you get financial worth and credibility as this is a decentralized currency and government can demonetizes your bitcoin as no one has control over it.	Bitcoin prices are very volatile and can increases or decreases at a very high pace.
On online purchases you enter your credit card number, debit card number and other information in a web form. There are chances of credit card number being stolen and much more. In case of bitcoin this does not happen as it happens with public key and private key. Your private key is secret.	Also used for money Laundering/Black Market.
Bitcoin is called the Future of Money as it is Non-Inflationary	Speculators wish to take advantages of Volatility of bitcoins. A huge recession will come in Bitcoins if it gets in the hands of speculator.
New bitcoins can be generated via a process called as mining. You can create bitcoins for yourself. Mining bitcoins through your computer	On loosing your bitcoin wallet, you lose all your bitcoins too. Backup phrase code can be used for recovering the bitcoin balance but as bitcoins are

gives you the power.	decentralized no one has control over it and you can't call any person/organization.
The transactions in the Bitcoin block chain can be verified by anyone making the information transparent.	Bitcoin is still at its infancy stage and is developing.
As there is public ledger, blockchains it is very hard to cheat or con anyone in Bitcoin. It gives freedom to merchants to do business with fewer risks.	Business can take benefit of bitcoins transaction but because of less awareness or lack of knowledgeable staff who understand digital currencies they won't guide their customers to use bitcoin transactions.

How Miners Create Coins And Confirm Transactions?

Let's have a look at the mechanism ruling the databases of cryptocurrencies. A cryptocurrency like Bitcoin consists of a network of peers. Every peer has a record of the complete history of all the transactions and thus of the balance of every account.

A transaction is a file that says, "Bob gives X Bitcoin to Alice" and is signed by Bob's private key. It's basic public key cryptography, nothing special at all. After signed, a transaction is broadcasted on the network, sent from one peer to every other peer. This is basic P2P-technology. Nothing special at all, again.

The transaction is known almost immediately by the whole network. But only after a specific amount of time it gets confirmed.

Confirmation is a critical concept in cryptocurrencies. You could say that cryptocurrencies are all about confirmation.

As long as a transaction is unconfirmed, it is pending and can be forged. When a transaction is confirmed, it is set in stone. It is no longer forgeable, it can't be reversed, it is part of an immutable record of historical transactions: of the so-called blockchain.

Only miners can confirm transactions. This is their job in a cryptocurrency-network. They take transactions, stamp them as legit and spread them in the network. After a transaction is confirmed by a miner, every node has to add it to its database. It has become part of the blockchain.

For this job, the miners get rewarded with a token of the cryptocurrency, for example with Bitcoins. Since the miner's activity is the single most important part of cryptocurrency-system we should stay for a moment and take a deeper look at it.

The central or general ledger works like a central repository that keeps records of transactions of a company's assets and liabilities, revenues, expenses, owner's equity, etc. In modern-day Enterprise Resource Planning software, this ledger will be the central ledger containing data sent from modules such as accounts payable, cash management, accounts receivable, projects and fixed assets. It, therefore, acts as the backbone of any accounting system and will bear both the organization's financial data and non-financial data. Every account in this ledger is referred to as a ledger account.

The central ledger is the source of financial position details and income statements. Every account will have a couple of pages, and the entries are referred to as journal entries that include both credits and debits. Any firm will have hundreds of accounts and many journal entries every year. This general ledger will generate the income statement, and this is why it is significant. It will give the details of cash flow and the balance sheet for the company. So, it is vital to keep the central ledger completely error-free and safe.

Initial Coin Offerings or ICOs are a popular way to finance cryptocurrency projects. In this event, the new cryptocurrency project will sell part of its tokens to the early birds in return for money. So, those creating these projects can use the ICOs to raise funds for their operations. They mostly use Bitcoin and such other cryptocurrencies. Before any project is done, the ICO takes place and it finances the expenses which are made by the founders for that project till it gets launched. Sometimes the ICO money may also be sent to a foundation where it is used to offer ongoing financial support to that project.

The ICOs today are being sold as software presale tokens and this is almost like giving an early access to a certain online game only to the early bird supporters. To prevent legal requirements associated with security sales, these ICOs today use terms like "crowdsale" and "donation" instead of the ICO. They also make sure that there are disclaimers to make participants aware that what they are doing is not a securities sale.

An initial coin offering (ICO) is a means by which funds are raised for a new cryptocurrency venture. An ICO may be used by startups with the intention of bypassing rigorous and regulated capital-raising processes required by venture capitalists or banks. However, securities regulators in many jurisdictions, including in the U.S., and Canada have indicated that if a coin or token is an "investment contract" (e.g., under the Howey test, i.e., an investment of money with a reasonable expectation of profit based significantly on the entrepreneurial or managerial efforts of others), it is a security and is subject to securities regulation. In an ICO campaign, a percentage of the cryptocurrency (usually in the form of "tokens") is sold to early backers of the project in exchange for legal tender or other cryptocurrencies, often bitcoin or Ether. The coins may ultimately be intended to be used as a medium of payment on a platform or serve some other purpose such as identity verification within an ecosystem.

Russian President Vladimir Putin has approved a timeline for a framework that will regulate initial coin offerings (ICO) and cryptocurrency mining operations.

This encompasses the life cycle of an ICO, from the original proposal of fundraising availability through to the most mature phase of trading on a cryptocurrency exchange (also known as "online trading platforms") ("exchange"). This is a high-level look above a market cap of $50M only, as an initial attempt to improve on the reporting we have seen to date on percentage failed ICO's. We will continue to develop our research in this area and produce a more in-depth study in coming months.

We break down ICO's into groups, with the following definitions:

- **Scam (pre-trading):** Any project that expressed availability of ICO investment (through a website publishing, ANN thread, or social media posting with a contribution address), did not have/had no intention of fulfilling project

development duties with the funds, and/or was deemed by the community (message boards, website or other online information) to be a scam.
- **Failed (pre-trading):** Succeeded to raise funding but did not complete the entire process and was abandoned, and/or refunded investors as a result of insufficient funding (missed soft cap).
- **Gone Dead (pre-trading):** Succeeded to raise funding and completed the process, however, was not listed on exchanges for trading and has not had a code contribution in Github on a rolling three-month basis from that point in time.
- **Dwindling (trading):** Succeeded to raise funding and completed the process, and was listed on an exchange, however had one or less of the following success criteria: deployment (in test/beta, at minimum) of a chain/distributed ledger (in the case of a base-layer protocol) or product/platform (in the case of an app/utility token), had a transparent project roadmap posted on their website, and had Github code contribution activity

in a surrounding three-month period ("Success Criteria").
- **Promising (trading):** Two of the above Success Criteria.
- **Successful (trading):** All of the above Success Criteria.

On the basis of the above classification, we found that approximately 81% of ICO's were Scams, ~6% Failed, ~5% had Gone Dead, and ~8% went on to trade on an exchange.

Bitcoin, Consensus term is often used in various ways. There are some rules in Bitcoin that are known as consensus rules which full nodes of Bitcoin have to consider when confirming a transaction on the network. For instance, consensus rules of Bitcoin need the blocks that create specific Bitcoins. In case, a block produces more than the required Bitcoins, then full nodes will not confirm the block and every miner had to accept it. Removal of consensus rule needs hardfork; whereas adding consensus rules is done by softfork. These rules are concerned only with transactions confirmation and blocks validation. If an economy disagrees with these rules, then economy and currency get separated into two independent pieces. In place of consensus rules, these rules can also be known as rules of Bitcoin or hard rules.

In addition, a consensus is also referred to as no objection among the people that matter. In case of Bitcoin, following consensus rules is much required; no section of Bitcoin can oppose hardfork. This agreement level is known as near-unanimous or non-contentious.

What Are Miners Doing?

Principally everybody can be a miner. Since a decentralized network has no authority to delegate this task, a cryptocurrency needs some kind of mechanism to prevent one ruling party from abusing it. Imagine someone creates thousands of peers and spreads forged transactions. The system would break immediately.

So, Satoshi set the rule that the miners need to invest some work of their computers to qualify for this task. In fact, they have to find a hash – a product of a cryptographic function – that connects the new block with its predecessor. This is called the Proof-of-Work. In Bitcoin, it is based on the SHA 256 Hash algorithm.

You don't need to understand the details about SHA 256. It's only important you know that it can be the basis of a Cryptologic puzzle the miners compete to solve. After finding a solution, a miner can build a block and add it to the blockchain. As an incentive, he has the right to add a so-called coinbase transaction that gives him a specific number of Bitcoins. This is the only way to create valid Bitcoins.

Bitcoins can only be created if miners solve a cryptographic puzzle. Since the difficulty of this puzzle increases the amount of computer power the whole miner's invest, there is only a specific amount of cryptocurrency token that can be created in a given amount of time. This is part of the consensus no peer in the network can break.

Revolutionary Properties:

If you really think about it, Bitcoin, as a decentralized network of peers which keep a consensus about accounts and balances, is more a currency than the numbers you see in your bank account.

What are these numbers more than entries in a database – a database which can be changed by people you don't see and by rules you don't know?

Basically, cryptocurrencies are entries about token in decentralized consensus-databases.

They are called CRYPTOcurrencies because the consensus-keeping process is secured by strong cryptography. Cryptocurrencies are built on cryptography. They are not secured by people or by trust, but by math. It is more probable that an asteroid falls on your house than that a bitcoin address is compromised.

Describing the properties of cryptocurrencies, we need to separate between transactional and monetary properties. While most cryptocurrencies share a common set of properties, they are not carved in stone.

Transactional Properties:

1.) **Irreversible**: After confirmation, a transaction can't be reversed. By nobody. And nobody means anybody. Not you, not your bank, not the President of the United States, not Satoshi, not your miner. Nobody. If you send money, you send it. Period. No one can help you, if you sent your funds to a scammer or if a hacker stole them from your computer. There is no safety net.

2.) **Pseudonymous**: Neither transactions, nor accounts are connected to real-world identities. You receive Bitcoins on so-called addresses, which are randomly seeming chains of around 30 characters. While it is usually possible to analyze the transaction flow, it is not necessarily possible to connect the real world identity of users with those addresses.

3.) Fast and global: Transaction is propagated nearly instantly in the network and is confirmed in a couple of minutes. Since they happen in a global network of computers, they are completely indifferent to your physical location. It doesn't matter if I send Bitcoin to my neighbor or to someone on the other side of the world.

4.) Secure: Cryptocurrency funds are locked in a public key cryptography system. Only the owner of the private key can send cryptocurrency. Strong cryptography and the magic of big numbers make it impossible to break this scheme. A Bitcoin address is more secure than Fort Knox.

5.) Permissionless: You don't have to ask someone to use cryptocurrency. It's just a software that everybody can download for free. After you installed it, you can receive and send Bitcoins or other cryptocurrencies.

No one can prevent you. There is no gatekeeper.

Monetary Properties:

1.) Controlled supply: Most cryptocurrencies limit the supply of the tokens. In Bitcoin, the supply decreases with time and will reach its final number somewhere in around 2140. All cryptocurrencies control the supply of the token by a schedule written in the code. This means the monetary supply of a cryptocurrency in every given moment in the future can roughly be calculated today. There is no surprise.

2.) No debt but bearer: The Fiat-money on your bank account is created by debt and the numbers, you see on your ledger represent nothing but debts. It's a system of IOU. Cryptocurrencies don't represent debts. They just represent themselves. They are money as hard as coins of gold.

To understand the revolutionary impact of cryptocurrencies, you need to consider both properties. Bitcoin as a permissionless, irreversible and pseudonymous means of payment is an attack on the control of banks and governments over the monetary transactions of their citizens. You can't hinder anyone to use Bitcoin, you can't prohibit someone to accept a payment, and you can't undo a transaction.

As money with a limited, controlled supply that is not changeable by a government, a bank or any other central institution, cryptocurrencies attack the scope of the monetary policy. They take away the control central banks take on inflation or deflation by manipulating the monetary supply.

What Is Cryptocurrency: 21st-Century Unicorn – Or The Money Of The Future?

This introduction explains the most important thing about cryptocurrencies. After you've read it, you'll know more about it than most other humans.

Today cryptocurrencies (Buy Crypto) have become a global phenomenon known to most people. While still somehow geeky and not understood by most people, banks, governments and many companies are aware of its importance.

In 2016, you'll had a hard time finding a major bank, a big accounting firm, a prominent software company or a government that did not research cryptocurrencies, publish a paper about it or start a so-called blockchain-project.

But beyond the noise and the press releases the overwhelming majority of people – even bankers, consultants, scientists, and developers – have a very limited knowledge about cryptocurrencies. They often fail to even understand the basic concepts.

So let's walk through the whole story. What are cryptocurrencies?

- **Where did cryptocurrency originate?**
- **Why should you learn about cryptocurrency?**
- **And what do you need to know about cryptocurrency?**

One of the interesting things about mining is that the difficulty of the puzzles is constantly increasing, correlating with the number of people trying to solve it. So, the more popular a certain cryptocurrency becomes, the more people try to mine it, the more difficult the process becomes.

A lot of people have made fortunes by mining Bitcoins. Back in the days, you could make substantial profits from mining using just your computer, or even a powerful enough laptop. These days, Bitcoin mining can only become profitable if you're willing to invest in an industrial-grade mining hardware. This, of course, incurs huge electricity bills on top of the price of all the necessary equipment.

Currently, Litecoins, Dogecoins, and Feathercoins are said to be the best cryptocurrencies in terms of being cost-effective for beginners. For instance, at the current value of Litecoins, you might earn anything from 50 cents to 10 dollars a day using only consumer-grade hardware.

But how do miners make profits? The more computing power they manage to accumulate, the more chances they have of solving the cryptographic puzzles. Once a miner manages to solve the puzzle, they receive a reward as well as a transaction fee.

As a cryptocurrency attracts more interest, mining becomes harder and the number of coins received as a reward decreases. For example, when Bitcoin was first created, the reward for successful mining was 50 BTC. Now, the reward stands at 12.5 Bitcoins. This happened because the Bitcoin network is designed so that there can only be a total of 21 million coins in circulation.

As of November 2017, almost 17 million Bitcoins have been mined and distributed. However, as rewards are going to become smaller and smaller, every single Bitcoin mined will become exponentially more and more valuable.

All of those factors make mining cryptocurrencies an extremely competitive arms race that rewards early adopters. However, depending on where you live, profits made from mining can be subject to taxation and Money Transmitting regulations. In the US, the FinCEN has issued a guidance, according to which mining of cryptocurrencies and exchanging them for flat currencies may be considered money transmitting. This means that miners might need to comply with special laws and regulations dealing with this type of activities.

The sudden increase in cryptocurrency mining has increased the demand for graphics cards (GPU) greatly. Popular favorites of cryptocurrency miners such as Nvidia's GTX 1060 and GTX 1070 graphics cards, as well as AMD's RX 570 and RX 580 GPUs, have all doubled if not tripled in price – or are out of stock completely. A GTX 1070 Ti which was released at a price of $450 is now being sold for as much as $1100.

Another popular card GTX 1060's 6 GB model was released at an MSRP of $250, but it is now being sold for almost $500. RX 570 and RX 580 cards from AMD are out of stock for almost a year now. Miners regularly buy up the entire stock of new GPU's as soon as they are available, further driving prices up. This has caused, in general, a disliking towards cryptocurrency miners by PC gamers and tech enthusiasts.

Nvidia is reportedly asking retailers to do what they can when it comes to selling GPUs to gamers instead of miners. "Gamers come first for Nvidia," said Boris Böhles, PR manager for Nvidia in the German region, in an interview with the German publication ComputerBase. "All activities around our GeForce products are for our core audience. We recommend our trading partners make arrangements to ensure that gamers' needs are still met in the current climate."

Cryptocurrencies: Dawn Of A New Economy

Mostly due to its revolutionary properties cryptocurrencies have become a success their inventor, Satoshi Nakamoto, didn't dare to dream of it. While every other attempt to create a digital cash system didn't attract a critical mass of users, Bitcoin had something that provoked enthusiasm and fascination. Sometimes it feels more like religion than technology.

Cryptocurrencies are digital gold. Sound money that is secure from political influence. Money that promises to preserve and increase its value over time. Cryptocurrencies are also a fast and comfortable means of payment with a worldwide scope, and they are private and anonymous enough to serve as a means of payment for black markets and any other outlawed economic activity.

But while cryptocurrencies are more used for payment, its use as a means of speculation and a store of value dwarfs the payment aspects.

Cryptocurrencies gave birth to an incredibly dynamic, fast-growing market for investors and speculators. Exchanges like Okcoin, poloniex or shapeshift enables the trade of hundreds of cryptocurrencies. Their daily trade volume exceeds that of major European stock exchanges.

At the same time, the praxis of Initial Coin Distribution (ICO), mostly facilitated by Ethereum's smart contracts, gave life to incredibly successful crowdfunding projects, in which often an idea is enough to collect millions of dollars. In the case of "The DAO", it has been more than 150 million dollars.

In this rich ecosystem of coins and token, you experience extreme volatility. It's common that a coin gains 10 percent a day – sometimes 100 percent – just to lose the same the next day. If you are lucky, your coin's value grows up to 1000 percent in one or two weeks.

While Bitcoin remains by far the most famous cryptocurrency and most other cryptocurrencies have zero non-speculative impact, investors and users should keep an eye on several cryptocurrencies. Here, we present the most popular cryptocurrencies of today.

BITCOIN

The one and only, the first and most famous cryptocurrency. Bitcoin serves as a digital gold standard in the whole cryptocurrency-industry, is used as a global means of payment and is the de-facto currency of cybercrime like Darknet markets or ransomware. After seven years in existence, Bitcoin's price has increased from zero to more than 650 Dollar, and its transaction volume reached more than 200.000 daily transactions.

There is not much more to say: Bitcoin is here to stay.

ETHEREUM

The brainchild of young crypto-genius Vitalik Buterin has ascended to the second place in the hierarchy of cryptocurrencies. Other than Bitcoin its blockchain does not only validate a set of accounts and balances but of so-called states. This means that Ethereum can not only process transactions but complex contracts and programs.

This flexibility makes Ethereum the perfect instrument for blockchain -application. But it comes at a cost. After the Hack of the DAO – an Ethereum based smart contract – the developers decided to do a hard fork without consensus, which resulted in the emerge of

Ethereum Classic. Besides this, there are several clones of Ethereum, and Ethereum itself is a host of several Tokens like DigixDAO and Augur. This makes Ethereum more a family of cryptocurrencies than a single currency.

RIPPLE

Maybe the less popular – or most hated – project in the cryptocurrency community is Ripple. While Ripple has a native cryptocurrency – XRP – it is more about a network to process IOUs than the cryptocurrency itself. XRP, the currency, doesn't serve as a medium to store and exchange value, but more as a token to protect the network against spam.

Ripple Labs created every XRP-token, the company running the Ripple network, and is distributed by them on will. For this reason, Ripple is often called pre-mined in the community and dissed as no real cryptocurrency, and XRP is not considered as a good store of value.

Banks, however, seem to like Ripple. At least they adopt the system with an increasing pace.

LITECOIN

Litecoin was one of the first cryptocurrencies after Bitcoin and tagged as the silver to the digital gold bitcoin. Faster than bitcoin, with a larger number of tokens and a new mining algorithm, Litecoin was a real innovation, perfectly tailored to be the smaller brother of bitcoin. "It facilitated the emergence of several other cryptocurrencies which used its codebase, but made it, even more, lighter". Examples are Dogecoin or Feathercoin.

While Litecoin failed to find a real use case and lost its second place after bitcoin, it is still actively developed and traded and is hoarded as a backup if Bitcoin fails.

MONERO

![Monero logo]

Monero is the most prominent example of the cryptonite algorithm. This algorithm was invented to add the privacy features Bitcoin is missing. If you use Bitcoin, every transaction is documented in the blockchain and the trail of transactions can be followed. With the introduction of a concept called ring-signatures, the cryptonite algorithm was able to cut through that trail.

The first implementation of cryptonite, Bytecoin, was heavily premined and thus rejected by the community. Monero was the first non-premined clone of bytecoin and raised a lot of awareness. There are several other incarnations of cryptonote with their own little improvements, but none of it did ever achieve the same popularity as Monero.

Monero's popularity peaked in summer 2016 when some Darknet markets decided to accept it as a currency. This resulted in a steady increase in the price, while the actual usage of Monero seems to remain disappointingly small.

Besides those, there are hundreds of cryptocurrencies of several families. Most of them are nothing more than attempts to reach investors and quickly make money, but a lot of them promise playgrounds to test innovations in cryptocurrency-technology.

What Is The Future Of Cryptocurrency?

The market of cryptocurrencies is fast and wild. Nearly every day new cryptocurrencies emerge, old die, early adopters get wealthy and investors lose money. Every cryptocurrency comes with a promise, mostly a big story to turn the world around. Few survive the first months, and most are pumped and dumped by speculators and live on as zombie coins until the last bagholder loses hope ever to see a return on his investment.

Markets are dirty. But this doesn't change the fact that cryptocurrencies are here to stay – and here to change the world. This is already happening. People all over the world buy Bitcoin to protect themselves against the devaluation of their national currency. Mostly in Asia, a vivid market for Bitcoin remittance has emerged, and the Bitcoin using darknets of cybercrime are flourishing. More and more companies discover the power of Smart Contracts or token on Ethereum, the first real-world application of blockchain technologies emerge.

The revolution is already happening. Institutional investors start to buy cryptocurrencies. Banks and governments realize that this invention has the potential to draw their control away. Cryptocurrencies change the world. Step by step. You can either stand beside or observe – or you can become part of history in the making.

Cryptocurrencies may have been little more than a hobby since their introduction in the late 1990s, but the technology's potential has finally started to catch the eye of mainstream financial institutions and professionals. The Winklevoss twins—famous for their involvement in Facebook Inc. - plan to launch the world's first Bitcoin exchange-traded fund (ETF) later this year, while the underlying technology has some of the world's largest banks filing a flurry of patents.

As Bitcoin's popularity grows, financial advisors are facing some tough questions and decisions from prospects and clients. They may explain the risks associated with these currencies and advice against them, but the decision is ultimately up to the client, and advisors should at least be familiar with how to identify and purchase cryptocurrencies. They should also be able to inform clients of any tax or legal issues surrounding cryptocurrencies in their jurisdiction.

In this article, we will take a look at cryptocurrencies like Bitcoin and what financial advisors need to know in order to best serve their clients. (For related reading, see: Risks and Rewards of Investing in Bitcoin.)

Cryptocurrency, Blockchain Technology

A cryptocurrency is a medium of exchange using cryptography to secure transactions and control the creation of units of currency. Unlike a central bank that print physical currency, cryptocurrencies rely on blockchain technology to decentralize the process. A blockchain is essentially a ledger that's kept by all participants in the market. When someone wants to add to it, these participants run algorithms to evaluate the proposed transaction and approve it.

In 2009, Bitcoin became the first major decentralized cryptocurrency in the market but faced a number of growing pains. Mt. Gox became the most popular Bitcoin exchange by 2013 - handling about 70% of all transactions - but the organization collapsed in early 2014 after 850,000 Bitcoins worth $450 million went missing. The currency also became infamous as a currency in the underground bazaar Silk Road before its shutdown.

Many other cryptocurrencies have sprung up since then, but Bitcoin remains the most popular with each BTC selling for about $546.10 as of Aug. 2, 2016. The ubiquity of the currency throughout the Internet has made it a popular alternative in countries where domestic currencies may be unstable or at risk for devaluation, while its maturity has made it a lot more reliable than many newer currencies that have struggled to gain traction. (For related reading, see: Bitcoin Tax Guide: Lost or Stolen Bitcoins.)

Bitcoins Pros and Cons

Cryptocurrencies may have a place in society's future, but that doesn't necessarily make them safe investments right now. In many ways, investing in these currencies now is akin to investing in an emerging market currency rather than the dollar or the euro. It might make sense as a speculative move, but the dramatic swings in value make it a sub-par currency for transactions, where stability is much more important than price appreciation.

Some Pros Of Cryptocurrencies Include:

- **Fraud:** Cryptocurrencies are impossible to counterfeit (unlike physical currencies) and cannot be reversed (like credit card chargebacks).
- **Settlement:** Cryptocurrency transactions are immediately settled without any third-party approvals (like credit cards) or contracts.
- **No fees:** Cryptocurrencies don't incur any transaction fees since the miners are compensated by the network (they're paid to verify transactions).

Some Cons Of Cryptocurrencies Include:

- **No security:** Cryptocurrencies can be electronically stolen and there is no recourse for the individual, unlike with a credit card.
- **Scalability:** There are a lot of questions about the scalability of cryptocurrencies on a technical level, which means they may be far off from replacing credit cards.
- **Applications:** There are relatively few merchants that accept Bitcoin payments

as of right now, which means the usefulness as a currency may be limited.

The Bottom Line

Cryptocurrencies have become very popular over the past several years, which means that financial advisors should be able to discuss them with their clients. Since these currencies are often highly speculative, advisors should make clients aware of the potential risks associated with them. They may also want to consult with an accountant or legal professional to determine if there are any other risks with using cryptocurrencies in their jurisdiction. (For related reading, see: Blockchain Company Files for New Bitcoin ETF.)

BLOCKCHAIN

A blockchain originally block chain is a continuously growing list of records, called blocks, which are linked and secured using cryptography. Each block typically contains a cryptographic hash of the previous block, a timestamp and transaction data. By design, a blockchain is inherently resistant to modification of the data. It is "an open, distributed ledger that can record transactions between two parties efficiently and in a verifiable and permanent way". For use as a distributed ledger, a blockchain is typically managed by a peer-to-peer network collectively adhering to a protocol for validating new blocks. Once recorded, the data in any given block cannot be altered retroactively without the alteration of all subsequent blocks, which requires collusion of the network majority.

Blockchains are secure by design and exemplify a distributed computing system with high Byzantine fault tolerance. Decentralized consensus has therefore been achieved with a blockchain. This makes blockchains potentially suitable for the recording of events, medical records, and other records management activities, such as identity management, transaction processing, documenting provenance, food traceability or voting.

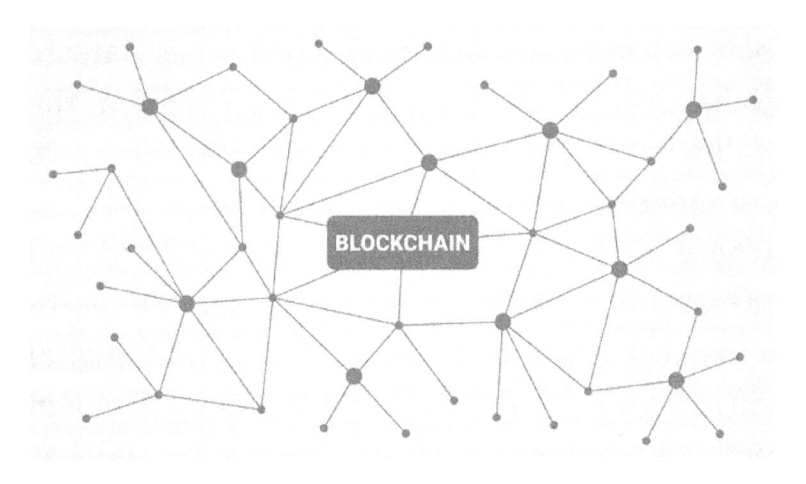

Blockchain was invented by Satoshi Nakamoto in 2008 for use in the cryptocurrency bitcoin, as its public transaction ledger. The invention of the blockchain for bitcoin made it the first digital currency to solve the double spending problem without the need of a trusted authority or central server. The bitcoin design has been the inspiration for other applications.

The first work on a cryptographically secured chain of blocks was described in 1991 by Stuart Haber and W. Scott Stornetta. In 1992, Bayer,

Haber, and Stornetta incorporated Merkle trees into the design, which improved its efficiency by allowing several documents to be collected into one block.

The first blockchain was conceptualized by a person (or group of people) known as Satoshi Nakamoto in 2008. It was implemented the following year by Nakamoto as a core component of the cryptocurrency bitcoin, where it serves as the public ledger for all transactions on the network.Through the use of a blockchain, bitcoin became the first digital currency to solve the double spending problem without requiring a trusted authority and has been the inspiration for many additional applications.

In August 2014, the bitcoin blockchain file size, containing records of all transactions that have occurred on the network, reached 20 GB (gigabytes). In January 2015, the size had grown to almost 30 GB, and from January 2016 to January 2017, the bitcoin blockchain grew from 50 GB to 100 GB in size.

The words block and chain were used separately in Satoshi Nakamoto's original paper, but were eventually popularized as a single word, blockchain, by 2016. The term blockchain 2.0 refers to new applications of the distributed blockchain database, first emerging in 2014. The Economist described one implementation of this second-generation programmable blockchain as coming with "a programming language that allows users to write more sophisticated, smart contracts, thus creating invoices that pay themselves when a shipment arrives or share certificates which automatically send their owners dividends if profits reach a certain level." Blockchain 2.0 technologies go beyond transactions and enable "exchange of value without powerful intermediaries acting as arbiters of money and information." They are expected to enable excluded people to enter the global economy, protect the privacy of participants, allow people to "monetize their own information," and provide the capability to ensure creators are compensated for their intellectual property. Second-generation blockchain technology makes it possible to store an individual's "persistent digital ID and persona" and provides an avenue to help solve the problem of social inequality by "potentially changing the way wealth is distributed".:14-15 As of 2016, blockchain 2.0 implementations continue to require an off-chain oracle to access any "external data or events based on time or market conditions [that need] to interact with the blockchain."

In 2016, the central securities depository of the Russian Federation announced a pilot project, based on the next blockchain 2.0 platforms that would explore the use of blockchain based automated voting systems. IBM opened a blockchain innovation research center in Singapore in July 2016. A working group for the World Economic Forum Meet in November 2016 to discuss the development of governance models related to blockchain. According to Accenture, an application of the diffusion of innovations theory suggests that blockchains attained a 13.5% adoption rate within financial services in 2016, therefore reaching the early adopter's phase. Industry trade groups joined to create the Global Blockchain Forum in 2016, an initiative of the Chamber of Digital Commerce.

Bitcoin Wallet

A Bitcoin wallet is a software program where Bitcoins are stored. To be technically accurate, Bitcoins are not stored anywhere; there is a private key (secret number) for every Bitcoin address that is saved in the Bitcoin wallet of the person who owns the balance. Bitcoin wallets facilitate sending and receiving Bitcoins and gives ownership of the Bitcoin balance to the user. The Bitcoin wallet comes in many forms; desktop, mobile; web and hardware are the four main types of wallets.

A Bitcoin wallet is also referred to as a digital Wallet. Establishing such a wallet is an important step in the process of obtaining Bitcoins. Just as Bitcoins are the digital equivalent of cash, a Bitcoin wallet is analogous to a physical wallet. But instead of storing Bitcoins literally, what is stored is a lot of relevant information like the secure private key used to access Bitcoin addresses and carry out transactions. The four main types of the wallet are desktop, mobile, web, and hardware.

Desktop wallets are installed on a desktop computer and provide the user with complete control over the wallet. Desktop wallets enable the user to create a Bitcoin address for sending and receiving the Bitcoins. They also allow the user to store a private key. A few known desktop wallets are Bitcoin Core, MultiBit, Armory, Hive OS X, Electrum, etc.

Mobile wallets overcome the handicap of desktop wallets, as the latter is fixed in one place. Once you run the app on your smartphone, the wallet can carry out the same functions as a desktop wallet, and help you pay directly from your mobile from anywhere. Thus a mobile wallet facilitates in making payments in physical stores by using "touch-to-pay" via NFC scanning a QR code. Bitcoin Wallet, Hive Android and Mycelium Bitcoin Wallet are few of the mobile wallets.

As for web wallets, they allow you to use Bitcoins from anywhere, on any browser or mobile. The selection of your web wallet must be done carefully since it stores your private keys online. Coinbase and Blockchain are popular web wallet providers.

The number of hardware wallets is currently very limited. These devices can hold private keys electronically and facilitate payments but are still in the development phase.

Keeping your Bitcoin wallet safe is very crucial. Some safeguards include: encrypting the wallet with a strong password, and choosing the cold storage option i.e. storing it offline.

How To Store

Unlike most traditional currencies, cryptocurrencies are digital, which entails a completely different approach, particularly when it comes to storing it. Technically, you don't store your units of cryptocurrency; instead, it's the private key that you use to sign for transactions that need to be securely stored.

There are several different types of cryptocurrency wallets that cater for different needs. If your priority is privacy, you might want to opt for a paper or a hardware wallet. Those are the most secure ways of storing your crypto funds. There are also 'cold' (offline) wallets that are stored on your hard drive and online wallets, which can either be affiliated with exchanges or with independent platforms.

Cryptocurrency Security

The security of cryptocurrencies is two parts. The first part comes from the difficulty in finding hash set intersections, a task done by miners. The second and more likely of the two cases is a "51%" attack. In this scenario, a miner who has the mining power of more than 51% of the network, can take control of the global blockchain ledger and generates an alternative block-chain. Even at this point, the attacker is limited to what he can do. The attacker could reverse his own transactions or block other transactions.

Cryptocurrencies are also less susceptible to seizure by law enforcement or having transaction holds placed on them from acquirers such as Paypal. All cryptocurrencies are pseudo-anonymous, and some coins have added features to create true anonymity.

Legality Of Cryptocurrencies

As cryptocurrencies are becoming more and more mainstream, law enforcement agencies, tax authorities and legal regulators worldwide are trying to understand the very concept of crypto coins and where exactly do they fit in existing regulations and legal frameworks.

With the introduction of Bitcoin, the first ever cryptocurrency, a completely new paradigm was created. Decentralized, self-sustained digital currencies that don't exist in any physical shape or form and are not controlled by any singular entity were always set to cause an uproar among the regulators.

A lot of concerns have been raised regarding cryptocurrencies' decentralized nature and their ability to be used almost completely anonymously. The authorities all over the world are worried about the cryptocurrencies' appeal to the traders of illegal goods and services. Moreover, they are worried about their use in money laundering and tax evasion schemes.

As of November 2017, Bitcoin and other digital currencies are outlawed only in Bangladesh, Bolivia, Ecuador, Kyrgyzstan, and Vietnam, with China and Russia being on the verge of banning them as well. Other jurisdictions, however, do not make the usage of cryptocurrencies illegal as of yet, but the laws and regulations can vary drastically depending on the country.

While cryptocurrencies are legal in most countries, Iceland and Vietnam are an exception

– Iceland, mainly due to their freeze on foreign exchange, they are not free from regulations and restrictions. China has banned financial institutions from handling bitcoins and Russia, while saying cryptocurrency is legal, has made it illegal to purchase goods with any currency other than Russian rubles.

In the U.S., the IRS has ruled that Bitcoin is to be treated as property for tax purposes, making Bitcoin subject to capital gains tax. The Financial Crimes Enforcement Network (FinCEN) has issued guidelines for cryptocurrencies. The issued guidelines contain an important caveat for Bitcoin miners: it warns that anyone creating bitcoins and exchanging them for fiat currency is not necessarily beyond the reach of the law. It states:

"A person that creates units of convertible virtual currency and sells those units to another person for real currency or its equivalent is engaged in transmission to another location and is a money transmitter."

Miners seem to fall into this category, which could theoretically make them liable for MTB classification. This is a bone of contention for bitcoin miners, who have asked for clarification. This issue has not been publicly addressed in a court of law to date.

Cryptocurrency Services

There are a host of services offering information and monitoring of cryptocurrencies. CoinMarketcap is an excellent way check on the market cap, price, available supply and the volume of cryptocurrencies. Reddit is a great way to stay in touch with the community and follow trends and CryptoCoinCharts is full of information ranging from a list of crytocoins, exchanges, information on arbitrage opportunities and more. Our very own site offers a list of crypto currencies and their change in value in the last 24 hrs, week or month.

Liteshack allows visitors to view the network hash rate of many different coins across six different hashing algorithms. They even provided a graph of the networks hash rate so you can detect trends or signs that the general public is either gaining or losing interest in a particular coin.

A hand website for a miner is CoinWarz. This site can help miners determine which coin is most profitable to mine given their hash rate, power consumption, and the going rate of the coins when sold for bitcoins. You can even view each coins current and past difficulty.

The United States Internal Revenue Service (IRS) ruled that bitcoin will be treated as property for tax purposes. This means bitcoin will be subject to capital gains tax. In a paper published by researchers from Oxford and Warwick, it was shown that bitcoin has some characteristics more like the precious metals market than traditional currencies, hence in agreement with the IRS decision even if based on different reasons.

The Cryptocurrency Alliance Super PAC. One of the many groups formed to protect consumer interests in cryptocurrencies.

In response to the IRS ruling, numerous organizations have been created to advocate for consumers. One of the most prominent examples is the Washington, D.C. based Cryptocurrency Alliance, an independent expenditure-only committee (Super PAC), created to raise awareness about cryptocurrencies and blockchain technology.

Legal issues not dealing with governments have also arisen for cryptocurrencies. Coinye, for example, is an altcoin that used rapper Kanye West as its logo without permission. Upon hearing of the release of Coinye, originally called Coinye West, attorneys for Kanye West sent a cease and desist letter to the email operator of Coinye, David P. McEnery Jr. The letter stated that Coinye was willful trademark infringement, unfair competition, cyberpiracy, and dilution and instructed Coinye to stop using the likeness and name of Kanye West. 17th of January 2014 Coinye was closed.

A primary example of this new challenge for law enforcement comes from the Silk Road case, where Ulbricht's bitcoin stash "was held separately and ... encrypted."

As the popularity of and demand for online currencies has increased since the inception of bitcoin in 2009, so have concerns that such an unregulated person to person global economy that cryptocurrencies offer may become a threat to society. Concerns abound that altcoins may become tools for anonymous web criminals.

Cryptocurrency networks display a marked lack of regulation that attracts many users who seek decentralized exchange and use of currency; however, the very same lack of regulations has been critiqued as potentially enabling criminals who seek to evade taxes and launder money.

Transactions that occur through the use and exchange of these altcoins are independent of formal banking systems and therefore can make tax evasion simpler for individuals. Since charting taxable income is based upon what a recipient reports to the revenue service, it becomes extremely difficult to account for transactions made using existing cryptocurrencies, a mode of exchange that is complex and (in some cases) impossible to track.

Systems of anonymity that most cryptocurrencies offer can also serve as a simpler means to launder money. Rather than laundering money through an intricate net of financial actors and offshore bank accounts, laundering money.

www.ingramcontent.com/pod-product-compliance
Lightning Source LLC
LaVergne TN
LVHW041623120325
805807LV00009B/245